Inspirational Parenting

Stories and Strategies for Parenting From the Heart

Kate Miller

BALBOA
PRESS
A DIVISION OF HAY HOUSE

ISBN: 978-1-4525-3700-9 (sc)
ISBN: 978-1-4525-3701-6 (e)

Balboa Press books may be ordered through booksellers or by contacting:

Balboa Press
A Division of Hay House
1663 Liberty Drive
Bloomington, IN 47403
www.balboapress.com
1-(877) 407-4847

Because of the dynamic nature of the Internet, any web addresses or links contained in this book may have changed since publication and may no longer be valid. The views expressed in this work are solely those of the author and do not necessarily reflect the views of the publisher, and the publisher hereby disclaims any responsibility for them.

The author of this book does not dispense medical advice or prescribe the use of any technique as a form of treatment for physical, emotional, or medical problems without the advice of a physician, either directly or indirectly. The intent of the author is only to offer information of a general nature to help you in your quest for emotional and spiritual well-being. In the event you use any of the information in this book for yourself, which is your constitutional right, the author and the publisher assume no responsibility for your actions.

Any people depicted in stock imagery provided by Thinkstock are models, and such images are being used for illustrative purposes only.
Certain stock imagery © Thinkstock.

Printed in the United States of America
Balboa Press rev. date: 8/8/2011

TABLE OF CONTENTS

Introduction
  Who Says Kids Don't Come with a Handbook? ix

Chapter One
  Forgiveness 1

Chapter Two
  The Role of Passion in Our Teen's Life 7

Chapter Three
  Embracing Uniqueness 13

Chapter Four
  Making Safe Decisions... 21

Chapter Five
  Unconditional Love and Perseverance – A
  Perfect Partnership.. 27

Chapter Six
  Children Learn What We Live 37

Chapter Seven
  I Believe In You.. 49

Chapter Eight
  Sometimes It Takes a Village to Save a Child 59

Chapter Nine
  Taking Care of You 69

Chapter Ten
  An Endless Stream of Hopes and Dreams 79

DEDICATION

Of all the beautiful moments I have had, and all that are to come, the greatest gift I have ever received is to be a mother.

Mac, Nan Loves You!

Mom, thank you for being my biggest fan.

Thank you Card, friends and family for your support

Cover by Artist Joan Marie I thank you dear friend.

My thanks to Kim and all at Theeverythingcompany. com.

Who Says Kids Don't Come with a Handbook?

Although there is humor and lightheartedness within the pages of this book, my desire to write parenting books comes from a much deeper place.

I had my first child when I was nineteen. He was the most beautiful child I had ever seen, and this feeling was accompanied by a love that was so deep it was a bit frightening. Over the course of ten years I had three children.

In this book I talk often about being a healthy parent. The qualities of a well-balanced parent set the stage for healthy parent/child adventures.

I was far from a well-balanced parent. This was, of course, not intentional. Yet my children, the very beings I loved more than life itself, experienced my lack of skills. I felt like I was placed in a job that was more important than any I could be given, without being able to read directions or ask for help.

My career working with children began many years ago, one job leading to the next, until I was working with kids and parents on a daily basis. It was in those countless hours of work that I truly understood what I believe to be great parenting.

I write parenting books to help parents who are searching for ideas to strengthen their experiences with themselves and their children. I write parenting books out of an endless love for all children. I am not a therapist and this is not therapy.

This book is here to give support to the tired heart and bring smiles to a child's face.

Today my children are young adults. They are among my heroes. They have built successful lives for themselves. They are kind and compassionate and make this world a better place. They are my favorite people to spend time with. I wish that I would have had this knowledge many years ago to fill the walls of our home. Today it is my joy to share what I have gathered with all who pick up this dear little book and read it.

Lovingly,
Kate

CHAPTER ONE

Forgiveness

Forgiveness is freedom. I believe it is important to address it at the beginning of this book. It lets go of the old and welcomes the new. Forgiveness never leaves us where it has found us and it is a vital part of parenting.

I can't count the number of teenagers who have sat in my office in tears because they needed their parents' forgiveness for something they had done. They explain, "I don't know how to move forward when my parents keep bringing up the past. I hate it that I hurt them, I cry at night when no one knows I'm crying. I would give anything to do that night over again." "I don't know what to do. When I look at my mom I feel so sad. When I wake up in the morning I think, 'please don't be sad today'. I want more than anything for my parents to be proud of me. I just want them to understand that I'm really sorry."

I was once asked by a mother, "Just how many times am I supposed to forgive my son?" I told her, "Always." Out of hundreds of teens I have worked with, I can't remember one child who was not sorry for hurting their parents for whatever reason. Most are willing to work very hard to regain that trust.

If you think about your teenagers and what they are trying to figure out right now, it makes it a bit easier to embrace forgiveness. We tell them to "grow up and be responsible" yet we also tell them that they are still children and they "*will* listen to what I have to say."

In my life, I have been hit hard with lessons of forgiveness. One of the dearest children I have ever had the joy of knowing was assaulted by an adult when she was nine. At night I cried until my eyes ached so badly I could not open them. This experience taught me very strong, valuable, and inspiring lessons. I hold on to these as my gifts from divine grace and I now refuse to allow the actions of others to take over my life. While this was an extreme situation, forgiveness, even in less complicated forms, is difficult work to do. But when it comes to raising our children we have no choice.

This is what I have learned about forgiveness: I am always in control of myself, my reactions, my words and thoughts, the mood I awake in each morning and the way I live each day. It is powerful to know we are always the ones making our decisions, not others or their actions. Forgiveness allows us to be in the present moment and to make fair and honest decisions.

When our teenagers make mistakes it is certainly necessary to have a discussion; however, make it a learning discussion. Instead of saying, "You are grounded for the next ten years. I told you to be home by ten, and it is midnight now. I can't believe how irresponsible you are. I am so disappointed in you," ask yourself "What is the real truth here?" Use this situation to talk about your *true feelings*: "I was so scared when you didn't come home. I had no idea where you were or if you needed my help. I was sure something had happened to you. I love you so much and I was really worried." Sharing your truth allows your child to understand that their decisions affect not only them but you as well. Anger was not the real cause of your reaction, fear was.

It is helpful to remember how you feel when you make a mistake. When I do something that upsets someone I care about, I know I want it to go away as quickly as possible. I don't want those around me reminding me of a mistake I made last month. I am certain I have done many wonderful things within the last month and I would love to hear about them. Our children are no different. If we take the time to look, we can find a lot of great and small things to praise our kids for. In order to go forward and be successful we cannot drag our past with us. It simply gets too heavy and we eventually stop moving. Our children are the same.

I once had a mother and daughter come to my office. They were living in the same house but not speaking to each other. The daughter was sixteen and had made some bad choices. She had stayed out all night, used drugs, missed countless days of school and her attitude during this time was less than attractive. She had called her mother horrible names and threatened to run away if she tried to "interfere." These events took place over a period of three months, during which time the daughter actually did run away. When she was ready to come home and start over, she didn't know how. The lessons she learned were painful. She was behind in school and had lost many of her friends. She felt ashamed and was sorry. She wanted and needed forgiveness so she could move forward.

As difficult as her pain was, her mother's was just as hard. "How can I ever trust her again? I know I can't live through that again, I just can't," she cried, tears streaming down her face. As a mother I felt her pain. But as someone who has worked with teens on a daily basis, I knew both she and her daughter needed a way out. I asked them to each make a list of the qualities they admired in each other and return to my office the next day. They were not to share their lists with each other until they were sitting in front of me, which wouldn't be hard because they were not speaking to each other.

The rule for our meeting the next day was, "We acknowledge there is a lot of pain, but we are willing to take a break, just for today." I asked them to read their lists, beginning with the daughter. She had over twenty lines of qualities she loved about her mother. Her mother also had a full list. I asked each of them to explain every quality in detail. It was a great day in my office. Tears ran like water and hearts opened, inviting forgiveness and setting the stage for new beginnings. They had to move from the mistakes to the healing. I wanted them to remember what it felt like to enjoy each other. The daughter opened up to the help she needed and her mother hung the list of qualities her daughter had written on her mirror, so she could see them every day. We worked from a place of joy, which allowed movement within a relationship that appeared frozen.

Teenagers are so amazing; they can have the worst day of their life on Thursday, and the best day on Friday. Perhaps there is a lesson in there for us all.

Forgiveness is a necessary quality to have when raising children. It blesses everyone, especially you!

Three Helpful Tools

1. Our teenagers need us, especially when they have made a mistake. Reach out in a way that lets them know you are still there. Go to dinner together and talk about good times you have shared. Write them a letter telling them you love them and

miss them. Leave work early and surprise them. There is an exercise I do that kids and parents love. Each of you write down what it is you are trying to forgive, say good bye to it, then toss it in the fireplace or throw it away. Once I got really creative and I had everyone write their thoughts down and stick them inside balloons and let them go. They watched their unhappy feelings float away. It was wonderful!

2. Take a few minutes to remember what it was like to be a teenager. The connection you will experience will be most helpful. Share it with your teen if it feels right to do so.

3. Sit quietly and remind yourself that each day is a new day as a parent and you are doing the best job you know how to do. Gather new energy; be excited you are learning. Praise is wonderful... for everyone!

Quotes

"Forgiveness is the fragrance that the violet sheds on the heal that has crushed it."
~ Mark Twain

"Man's deepest need and highest achievement is forgiveness."
~ Horace Bushnell

"Removing anger makes room for grace and forgiveness."
~ Kate Miller

Affirmation

I honor who you are. Every time I think of you
I see beauty and wholeness. I love you.

A space for you to write your own affirmation

CHAPTER TWO

The Role of Passion in Our Teen's Life

Passion is described in Roget's Thesaurus as intensity, enthusiasm, burning desire, eagerness, exuberance and spirit.

As parents we want to give our kids safe, successful and happy futures. It is also nice to believe that some of the knowledge we have gained in our lifetime is important to share. However, the way we offer our knowledge makes all the difference in the world.

Helping our teens discover their passion is a great journey to take together. The focus and energy that comes with this is amazing. I have many exciting cases where passion has been the saving grace of a child. The following story happens to be one of my favorites.

There have been stories for years about the magic of girls and their horses. Most horse people say it has to do with a girl being in control of something so much bigger than she is. There is an unexplainable trust and devotion between them. They look out for one another. They are friends. It is the story of my oldest daughter. I often heard my daughter speak of her horses as being "honest". I have witnessed first-hand the beauty of such relationships.

One afternoon I ran into my daughter's bus driver at the grocery store. "How is your daughter feeling?" he inquired. "I guess she must really have what's going around. I haven't seen her for a week now."

I thought the bus driver must be crazy! I raced home and asked my daughter, "How was school?" "I hated it just like I do every other day," she replied. After I stopped shaking and maintained my meltdown I sat beside her. "I want to know what is going on, really going on. Where you have been?" My daughter cried. She told me that she would hide behind the library when the bus would drive up and after it left she would ride the city bus to the mall with a girl she had met at school. This is a child who had never been in trouble. She liked school, worked hard, and made good grades. She explained that there was an empty feeling that was with her a lot. "I have never been this lonely in my whole life, mom," she said. Looking into her eyes, I knew this was true. At that moment I believed our empty feelings may have been equal.

As her mother, it was my responsibility to keep her safe and provide opportunities that offered success and happiness. I thought my heart was going to break. "What should I do?" I asked myself. This is the answer that I heard, and I heard it very clearly: "Ask her this: 'If you could do anything in the world, what would you do? How can I help you?'" This question was not about school, or the lessons she had missed. I was not angry with my daughter; I was scared. I was asking her with my whole heart, "How can I help?" I knew intuitively that inside my daughter she had the answer. Without hesitation, she replied, "Please mom, help me be with horses, help me find a place where I can be with animals. My whole life I've wanted to ride horses. Nothing else feels good to me, nothing." (I want to be clear that this was *not* a case of a young girl who didn't get her way about something and refused to do as she was asked.)

I was a single mom with a lot of responsibility and my daughter had never shied away from making this task easier for me. She helped out at times when most others wouldn't even notice there was a need. I had no idea how I was going to pull it off, but I had faith in my love for my daughter and nothing was going to stop me from listening to, and acting on, this heartfelt request.

"Before tomorrow ends, I promise you I will find you a horse to ride," I vowed. I never doubted that I would fulfill that wish. It was part of who my daughter was and her need to fill that void would be met. She would not have had this strong desire if it was not meant to be. My part was to take action. (Remember, in the introduction to this book, I said that "love" is an action word - this is exactly what that means.)

I called four barns in our area inquiring about lessons for my daughter. The first three places I called I could not have paid for lessons even if I had sold my one hundred-year-old car! But the fourth... Aha! An amazing woman gave my daughter the opportunity to live her passion. She became a "working student" working after school (and yes, she returned to school) in exchange for lessons. And my daughter worked hard... in winter, during the rains, after dark... and never, not ever, did she complain. She groomed horses that belonged to girls her age that cost more than the money some people make in a year. Still, she groomed with a smile on her face, embracing each and every horse. It was her passion, her reason for being. In some wonderful and magical way, when I would watch my daughter ride, I would think, "Wow. She is so one with that horse. They are so well-balanced I don't know where one begins and the other ends."

Horses and her new friends at the barn became her life. She was successful and happy, and her passion escorted her all through school, even offering her the opportunity to travel and have great adventures. These wonderful memories that I will hold in my heart forever began with my daughter's dream, a passionate feeling unique to her heart only. Her job was to live her passion and mine was to help her achieve it. Nothing can stand between your teen and their passion. I think of myself as an instrument in a child's own symphony, striving to add harmony to their masterpiece and dancing to their tune.

Teenagers want to feel good about what they do. They need praise. They want to feel love and success and be noticed. They need encouragement and they want us to believe in them. Relationships with our children give true meaning to the term "unconditional love". At times we need to be very active, taking action. Other times our support can be silent, holding them deep within our hearts and standing in awe of what they are learning.

Three Helpful Tools

1. It is helpful to remember that your child's passion is a part of them. It is as connected to them and as purposeful as their legs are for running.

2. Our responsibility as parents is to offer opportunity and support. Visit the book store with your child. Ask them to write down five ways you can help them learn more about their passion.

3. Be interested; get excited about this adventure. Even though it is their passion, they need you and your energy. Have fun!

Quotes

(Passion is) "…energy that boils over,
running down the sides of the pot."
~ Arnold Glason

(Passion is) "…fire under control."
~ Norman Vincent Peale

"It is impossible to separate a person from
their passion. They are one."
~ Kate Miller

Affirmation

I believe in you and your passion in
life. I lovingly support you.

A space for you to write your own affirmation

CHAPTER THREE

Embracing Uniqueness

This book began about fourteen years ago. I was working for our local police department as an on-site counselor. The mission of the program I was working with was to meet with teenagers on an individual basis. We discussed the reason for their arrest and replaced a court visit with six months of creative planning, individualized to meet their needs. It was my job and my pleasure to establish a relationship with them and offer them opportunities to make successful and healthy decisions. We spent long hours discovering where their interests lie and how to get them there. I told all of my kids the same thing. "It doesn't matter to me what you have done up to this moment. What matters to me is where we go from here." I was part of the police department for nine years and saw hundreds of teenagers, each with their own unique story. I would like to share a few of their stories with you. It is because of these experiences that I use the term "Embracing Uniqueness".

The chief of police often asked me to spend Friday nights downtown getting to know our local teens. I found it exciting and, on one particular occasion, very humbling. While walking on Main Street around 8:30 p.m. one evening I noticed a group of five teenagers walking toward me. They were loud and covered with tattoos. They were wearing black makeup, strange hairstyles, and chains that appeared heavy enough to tow a large truck. I crossed the street to avoid my discomfort, which was escalating quickly. They didn't look like the teenagers I was used to seeing locally and my desire to reach out was overcome by my discomfort. The rest of the night was a typical Friday night, talking with our local kids. Driving home that evening, I thought to myself, "What a relief that I didn't run into that peculiar group of five again." Or so it seemed.

As I entered through the door of the police department early Monday morning, I saw five citations on my desk. "Hmm, a group of five?" I thought. I had a light-hearted laugh when I thought of a group this large all getting citations; most of the time at least one of them gets away. One of the officers told me that all five kids had come to the department asking for me early that morning. My name was on the citation they had been given at the time of the arrest; most kids, however, waited for me to call. Very few would be in a hurry to pay a visit to the police department. "And wait 'til you see these five. I don't think they live around here," was the officer's comment. As I walked to the reception area, who was waiting for me but my five interesting characters from Friday night? It appears that my technique of avoidance had been a temporary one.

I felt a bit uncertain for a moment, again focusing on their appearance, as I invited them back to my office. My office was an average size, so six people made for close quarters. There I sat, wondering what to say or where to start. I asked myself why I was so uncomfortable with this group of kids. As I stepped over a large black boot to reach my desk, I noticed that one of the boys had gone to great lengths to move both himself and his chair so that I would not be inconvenienced by the crowded room. Then, to my even bigger surprise, the young man closest to me pulled out my chair. "Well I don't believe this has happened in this office before," I said. They all smiled, and I noticed how their faces softened.

The leader of the group spoke first. His hair stood about six inches off his head in a Mohawk that was so sharp on its ends I believe it could have cut wood, and was a bright shade of blue that went nicely with his chains and multiple piercings. I asked him to explain to me, if he didn't mind, how one got one's hair so precise. He and the rest of the group were very happy to share their expertise. I gained great knowledge in how to style a Mohawk. You never know when this information might come in handy. He asked me several intelligent questions about the citations they had received as I listened curiously. Then I began to ask each member of the group the same questions I asked all youths who ended up in my office: "Where do you live?" "Who do you live with?" "How did you end up in this situation?" "How can I help?"

Their answers to these questions brought tears to my eyes. These kids were between fifteen and eighteen years old. Three of them lived wherever they could find a place to stay; one lived with her mother and the other in a garage. Only one of these kids had a parent who cared about her but whose parenting skills were very limited. The young boy who stayed in his aunt's garage was not allowed in the house; his dad was in jail and his aunt was angry that she had to watch her brother's children. She focused her anger on this boy. He would not leave because his younger sister lived there and he wanted to be sure she was safe and went to school every day. Out of these five children, there were no dads interested or available. Two of my young men thought their dads might be in prison, but since they had been abandoned by their mothers, they had very little information. They worked odd jobs and shared with each other whatever they were given. They had formed a family, and their devotion to each other was heartfelt. By the end of our hour-long interview I was filled with admiration, thinking long and hard about my initial judgment. I did not feel good about myself.

Over the next several months we became very good friends. We established a specific schedule for them to follow and they followed it perfectly. I learned about their dreams and their passions. We found classes they could take to begin building their education. I had one young man who deeply wanted to find a relative... any relative. We found his uncle and I invited him to my office. He had no idea he had a nephew, and a wonderful nephew at that. This boy's uncle and I made it possible for the group to rent rooms so they could have a place to call home. These amazing survivors taught me the meaning of judgment. My prayer was simply to remember this story for the rest of my life: "Please help me embrace the uniqueness within each child who crosses my path, to see with my heart first and not my eyes. Please don't let one opportunity pass by that I may reach out to a sweet soul whose life I have the honor of making a little better." I am happy to say that we stayed in touch for the next two years, and they will live in my heart forever.

As parents we have our own ideas of what things should look like. Often we are called on to embrace uniqueness in our children that we don't understand but that our children see as completely wonderful. The word *embrace* means "to hold, to envelop, to hang onto, to not let go of".

I once met a young man who was fifteen years old and an excellent student. He was brilliant both academically and musically. He had loving parents who had supported his every step. He was at the top of his class in elementary school and did well in middle school. As his freshman year began his mother noticed a change taking place. He wasn't funny anymore. He did not appear happy about attending school. He was stressed from the amount of work he was being given in high school, though his study habits remained strong. He continued to demonstrate the same self-discipline he'd always had. He tried to talk with his parents about alternative schools. He was very excited about a school he had found within driving distance. It had a large music program as well as strong academics. The school was a bit more easy-going with its students and took into consideration the pace at which they were most comfortable performing while maintaining high standards. This school had a more personal touch. It was a smaller semi-private school and could provide individual attention that some larger schools are not able to offer.

This boy's parents had graduated from his current high school as had many family members. They had talked about and planned for their son to follow in their footsteps. His dad was good friends with the principal and his mother was a member of PTA. The thought of their son leaving that school was not a discussion they were willing to have. As time passed, their communication degraded. The communication that had once been open and safe now felt tense and confined. Embracing uniqueness would become a very valuable tool!

The parents asked if they could come and talk with me. They wanted to know if I would convince their son that he would be making a mistake by leaving their beloved high school. I said I would be happy to talk with their son, but first wanted to hear about their memories of high school. We met and they talked for an hour. Each parent was so filled with enthusiasm that they completed each other's sentences. **"Remember the time the gym flooded? Our class spent every weekend for six months raising money to cover the repairs. That was the best example of team work we have**

ever known. To this day we both have great friends because of that flood."

I said, "I am thrilled that you had this kind of experience in high school. All kids should. I know if your son could accomplish this in his current school he would. I know your goal for him is to create wonderful memories, but he isn't, and he's asking you for help. Ask him why he feels the school he has found would work better for him."

"Listen to him," I continued, "not with disappointment but with openness. Embrace him and his uniqueness. Reassure him that together you will find an answer. Enter this conversation with love; trust the great parenting you have given him. He has been asking for your help; he values your support. You have given him the courage to ask for what he needs. Now listen with your hearts. Embrace his uniqueness. Both of you are creative, loving parents. I know you can do this."

Just because their high school had worked for them did not mean it would work for their son. They called me the next day to tell me they had an appointment to visit the school their son was so excited about. They felt relief because they had given themselves permission to think differently. They were happy about the conversation that had taken place with their son. This young student did eventually change schools and graduated with honors.

If you can see your child's uniqueness and embrace it, you will be amazed at the transformation that will take place for all of you.

Three Helpful Tools

1. When your children were little you embraced them, even when they were kicking and screaming. They are still your children; they just don't fit on

your lap anymore and challenges seem bigger. When doing conflict resolution for schools I often ask students and parents what they are trying to accomplish and remind everyone we are all on the same team. One great tool is for each person to make a list establishing what they want the outcome to be, then meet each other on the fifty yard line. Writing things down helps to organize ideas so everyone involved can see what needs to be done. This also allows parents and teens to notice when the other is offering some form of compromise. Often once things are in front of us in writing it is much easier to work out details.

2. Communication between you and your teen is a gift. If they let you into their world, be patient; answers will come. The term *unconditional love* was coined by the parent of a teen. I have learned, after spending hundreds of hours with teenagers, that they are listening - even when we think they are not. They do value your opinions; give them some time to think. If you have been at an impasse, do something completely unrelated to the problem. Change the atmosphere. Rent your favorite movie and share with them your favorite parts. Go out to dinner and just enjoy the food.

3. Don't be afraid to ask for help. Go to your child's school and request a meeting with a counselor. They have great knowledge of what is happening with teens. Never think you are lacking in your skills just because you ask for help.

Quotes

*"The greatness of art is not to find what is
common, but what is unique."*

~ Anonymous

*"Today you are you, that is truer than true. There
is no one alive who is Youer than You."*

~ Dr. Seuss

*"Every color, shape and size is needed in
the garden to create beauty.
It is the uniqueness of each flower that holds its power."*

~ Kate Miller

Affirmation

The uniqueness of who you are is your
gift - I love you and support you.

A space for you to write your own affirmation

CHAPTER FOUR

Making Safe Decisions

One of the great challenges we face as parents is to hold tight when our children disagree with our decisions. It gets even harder when they strongly disagree. It's fair to say that many a parent's mind has been changed by pure and simple fatigue. We have such a strong desire to please our children that we often make decisions from a place of sentiment instead of safety. While working for the police department I met with parents daily who said, "I wish I would have stayed with my original decision. I knew I should have said no." These were wonderful parents with wonderful kids. If, after doing your homework regarding your son's or daughter's request, you still feel something isn't right, believe in You! Below are two examples of how to handle this dilemma. One is of a parent coming from a place of emotion ("caving in") and the second is of a parent coming from a place of safety.

Example One

> Parent: "Honey, I don't feel good about you going to the party tonight. I have no idea who Steve is or where he lives."

> Teen: "Everyone is going to be there."

Parent: "That still doesn't tell me who Steve is."

Teen: "He's in my English class. I've talked about him a hundred times. Josh can pick me up, mom. You don't even have to drive."

Parent: "Do you have an address?"

Teen: "Yeah, it's over by Michael's Market. Josh knows how to get there. Come on, mom. Are you trying to ruin my life here?"

Parent: "Of course not. I want you to be with your friends and have fun."

Teen: "So it's good then. I can go?"

Parent: "I'm still not feeling comfortable about this with so little information."

Teen (in a very loud voice): "I can't believe this. I can't wait until I can move out of here. You don't care about my feelings at all."

Parent: "Of course I do. I'm sorry you're so upset. You say Josh is going and Steve lives over by Michael's Market?" (At this point the parent is starting to cave.)

Teen: "Yes, and you can trust me, mom. Honest. If you let me go, you are the best mom in the whole world." (Then mom gets flashed that smile that melts her heart and she has just lost this one.)

Parent: "Okay, but be home by 11:00."

Teen: "How about 12:00?"

The above child had one goal and one goal only: To get to that party.

Because this parent was coming from a place of emotion she didn't stand a chance. The focus should have been on the safety of the party. Instead the focus was placed on the parent and how "mean" the parent was. Because sentiment was in control, the unhappiness the teen displayed was very uncomfortable. It's natural to want our children to be happy so we adjust our true feelings to comply with their immediate desires. (I used to be the queen of sentiment with my children.)

Take a moment and think about the depths you have gone to, insuring your child's safety. When your child was an infant you had their very life in your hands. As they began to walk you moved anything in their path that could cause harm. You waited for the school bus side by side and made sure they were dressed warmly enough. It is simply impossible to count the hours you have spent ensuring their protection.

Now let's look at the same situation, this time basing the decision on the safety of the child.

Example Two

> Teen: "Mom, there's this great party at Steve's house tonight. Can I go?"

> Parent: "Who is Steve? Will his parents be there?"

> Teen: "Oh, he's in my English class; you've heard me talk about him a hundred times."

> Parent: "Will his parents be home? Where does he live? If you give me a number I will be happy to call."

> Teen: "Oh my gosh, you have got to be kidding. That is the most embarrassing thing you could possibly do to me. Don't you trust me?"

Parent: "Of course I trust you, but I don't know Steve or his parents. If I don't know them and you don't want me to call, then I don't feel comfortable with you going to this party. This isn't about trust for me; this is about your safety."

Teen: "I can't believe you. I can't wait until I'm old enough to move out. Everybody will be there but me. Why are you doing this?"

Parent: "I'm doing this because I believe it is the safest decision I can make. I'm sorry if you're upset, but I would rather you are upset with me than to agree to something I do not feel good about. It's my job to keep you safe and that is what I am going to do. If you would like to have some friends over tonight I'd be happy to rent movies and buy pizza for you."

Teen leaves the room and slams the door.

Often, after a few hours have passed, the idea of pizza and movies can sound pretty inviting. But even if your kind offer isn't accepted, your child will forgive you. You have taken a stand for their safety and kids, even if they can't express it at the time, need and appreciate these boundaries. It is our job as parents to keep our children safe, even if we lack popularity for a few days.

Three Helpful Tools

1. It is very helpful to have house rules established ahead of time around the events you know will be repeated throughout your teen's years. The above problem could have been easily avoided

if rules were in place. Here are a few of the most common rules that need to be in place before the event occurs:

What time is curfew?

What is our house rule about attending parties?

What time is homework time?

Can I go out on a school night?

Who can I ride with? (If friends are old enough to drive.)

Do you need to know the parents if I'm spending the night?

What have we decided about dating?

What are my responsibilities at home? (i.e. washing dishes, washing car, cleaning room)

These important agreements establish order, safety and boundaries within families.

1. Make your house rules together. I have many families of teens who have great discussions while doing this. It also allows you to hear what is really important to your teen.

2. I have interviewed hundreds of kids when working in our high schools on the topic of parties. After gathering hours of what I believe to be very accurate information from teenagers I have a simple and safe party rule: No parent, no party. It is so important to follow what you know

is right. Some of my most courageous moments were accompanied by shaking knees.

Quotes

"If a child can't learn the way we are teaching them, maybe we should teach them the way they learn."
~ Ignacio Estrada

"Sooner or later all children quote their parents."
~ Bern Williams

"A perfect day does not make a perfect parent. Love, courage, faith and perseverance... these all live within amazing parents."
~ Kate Miller

Daily Affirmation

I love the understanding and respect we have for each other. I hold you in a place of safety and joy.

A space for you to write your own affirmation

CHAPTER FIVE

Unconditional Love and Perseverance – A Perfect Partnership

Love: *Devotion, fondness, affection, adoration, yearning, loyalty, passion, attachment, tenderness, all embracing.* These are just a few definitions of the word love.

Unconditional: *Without limits, unrestricted, boundless and immeasurable.* When you think of unconditional love, you begin to grasp the power it holds.

Perseverance: *To continue in spite of, to carry on, hang on, press on, hang tough, proceed.*

When I think of a parent's love for their children what comes to mind is the word "active". I once met with a mother who was questioning her love for her daughter: "I have been hurt so much; I just don't think I can take much more. There are days when I wake up and think I have no love left, I am finished." I asked her why she had come to my office and she said, "It is one of the many stops I am making today." She had gone to her daughter's school to drop off lunch money and taken her daughter's personal information to her new employer so she could begin her after-school job. Now she was sitting in my office scheduling an appointment so they could begin to work on their relationship. I assured her she had plenty of love left, pointing out all of the kind things she had done for her daughter and it wasn't even noon. After working with hundreds of parents and teens I am convinced that their love for each other is never lost, but they do get tired and frightened. These feelings drain energy and lead nowhere.

What do you do when you find yourself feeling this way? The word that comes to my mind is "perseverance". Let's think about this word as it pertains to life. Anything that we want to accomplish takes perseverance. I wanted to return to college after I had my children. What an undertaking! Day after day I asked myself, "What am I doing? This is so hard!" But a wonderful voice would speak to my heart, and every time I felt overwhelmed I was rescued by the following thought: "You are doing this to give yourself and your children a better life." That was all I needed to hear; it was my magic thought.

I've always loved the part in Peter Pan when Tink begins to fade away and she says, "Clap your hands if you believe in fairies and I will live." Many times in my career I have felt like clapping hands for teenagers and parents, knowing that the love and support they desire is there, it just feels buried underneath hurt feelings.

I would like to share with you a short story about the importance of perseverance. There was a man who was determined to have the best garden in town. He bought very expensive seeds to plant and waited for just the right moment for planting. He dug deep into the soil and placed each seed carefully into its hole. He took his hands and gently placed the soil over the seeds. He then waited for his crop to grow. Each morning he ran to his garden to see if the seeds had grown. "Grow, grow!" he told his garden, yet as days passed nothing happened. "Maybe I should yell louder," he thought. "GROW, GROW you darn seeds, what more do you want?" The neighbor next door heard him yelling. He suggested he water the seeds and pull the weeds. "The work has just begun," his neighbor said. "Now you have to be available for all the needs your garden might have." "No one told me that! This is much harder than I thought," said the man. He did want his garden to be beautiful so he took his neighbor's advice. First his tomatoes were attacked by tomato worms. Down to the store he went, searching for the best way to get the bugs out of his garden.

Next there was a huge rain storm and the man had to go out in the middle of the night to dig trenches so his vegetables would not drown. As if that wasn't enough, he was called out of town for several days and had to pay someone to come in and tend to his garden's needs. He got home only to find that one of his plants was in direct sunlight and, as the summer days grew warmer, he needed to build something to offer shade. The man began to notice that his garden responded to the amount of attention he was giving it. The previously weak plants now stood strong and green.

At the time of harvest he was so thrilled by the beauty of his vegetables that he wanted to share them with all of his neighbors. After the feast had ended the man sat next to his garden thinking of all the long hours of work it had taken to produce such lovely vegetables. "I am happy that my plants didn't grow just by my command, for I would have never really gotten to know their needs," thought the man. "It was in the dark of night, while the rain poured down on me, that I felt closest to my garden, fighting for its survival. I would not have had it any other way." Through perseverance the man realized his unconditional devotion to his garden.

I wrote that story after struggling to find words that explain the importance of perseverance when working with teens.

There are days when we ask ourselves, "What should I do next? I have tried everything and nothing seems to be working." I believe this is the time that you become an active listener. We have millions of ideas running through our minds at any given moment. Listen! What do you hear that will embrace what is happening for you and your child right now? I love the question, "What is my highest sense of right?" I use it all the time when faced with decisions. It takes thinking to a higher place. It makes you search for the best possible answer. I have worked with many families who have found that extra bit of patience for their teen by thinking from this place. I want to add that when we search for the best possible answer to support our child's need, we are always blessed by the outcome! I love the old saying, "What blesses one blesses all." I find it to be very true.

Unconditional love is called upon in many different ways. If one makes an effort to connect to its power it will take him on wonderful adventures. Years ago I associated the words unconditional love with my own children. I now know it has a far greater meaning. The only limits love knows are the ones we give it. The following story is the best explanation I know of unconditional love. It changed my life.

While I was working as a counselor for the police department an officer brought in a juvenile, age fourteen, to my office. She was kicking and screaming. She hated everyone, especially me. Within the first three minutes of our introduction she explained to me that she hated my color, my clothes, and my job. "Looking at your face makes me want to throw up." I asked her to have a seat so she stood. I ask her to stop yelling and swearing so she refused to talk. She was dirty and desperately needed a bath. There was not one sign of softness to her, inside or out. I got very quiet and asked myself, "Where do I go from here?" Since she was a juvenile I could not release her until I located a parent. "Who shall I call to pick you up? I think it best if we meet tomorrow after you have had time to calm down a bit. All of this can be very frightening." "No one!" was her reply. "You can call no one, not one person in the world, no one, not one person, do you hear me? NO ONE!" The pain in her eyes pierced my soul. I suddenly realized she was all alone. There was no one to call.

"What a huge world to be alone in. You are so brave. How do you do it? You are so young! I so admire you. I would be scared and I'm an adult." There was a long pause and then her eyes filled with tears that she did not acknowledge, and out of respect for her, neither did I. "I just handle it whatever way I can." She spoke!

"Well, if you don't mind I'd like to give you my phone number, then we have someone you can call." "That's crazy. Your sittin' right here," she retorted. "Here is the number to my phone, this one, right here on my desk, and here is my cell phone. You can call me." I looked at her as she sat down across from me, and she smiled just the smallest of smiles. "Hi, I'm Kate and I'm so happy to meet you. I was just sitting here hoping something exciting would happen today and in you walked. Thank you."

Over the course of the next few weeks I learned a lot about the life of my new friend. She was kicked out of her house by her mother when she turned fourteen. Her mother was not well and felt her daughter was a great burden. She had a grandfather who was so mean *I* was scared of him. She didn't know where her dad was but she was one of many children he had fathered. She described dragging the kitchen chair to the stove so she could cook noodles and rice for her mother. She had been making their dinner since she was five. "Why didn't you ask a teacher for help, or someone, anyone?" I asked. "I was scared they would take me away and then who would cook for my mom?" she relied.

I spent the next eight years with this wonderful young girl. Together we found her different places to stay until she was sixteen. At that time we filed for her to be emancipated by the court. She could not rent an apartment or even a room under her own name unless she was emancipated. She had a part time job and was taking classes to make up for the years of school she had missed. I had the joy of giving her her first birthday party and introducing traditions into her life. We celebrated Christmas together. She had her first Thanksgiving dinner and we shopped for her school needs together. She learned about values, loving herself, making healthy choices, and most importantly, having the courage to dream. I was able to get sponsors for her educational needs and my family and friends grew to love her.

I remember when she rented her first apartment. It was about 10:00 p.m. and my phone rang. "I'm scared, Kate. This place is strange and scary. Can you come and get me?" she asked. I had known her for a long time by now so I said, "Of course I will come get you. But you used to live under the bridge! How you can be scared in your own apartment?" "Yeah, I know, but that felt comfortable. This is strange and I feel so lonely," she answered. My sweet friend stayed with me for the next few nights until she felt safe in her new home.

We had a wonderful party when she got her GED and again when she passed her test to be a personal assistant. I fought for her rights like I would fight for my own children. She *was* one of my children. She is everyone's child. Over the past few years I have not seen much of my friend, and for good reasons. She has a good job and a nice boyfriend. When I last spoke to her she had moved back home to live with her mother, the same person who had abandoned her, had left her alone in the cold. When she told me I was frozen with fear. "What? How did that happen? Is she good to you, are you safe?" I asked. She smiled and gave me a giant hug. "She needs someone to cook for her Kate, and take care of her. After all, she is old now and she's my mother. I'm doin' good Kate, I really am. I'm happy and I'm doin' good." This dear girl taught me the meaning of unconditional love!

Unconditional love is your right as a parent, as a person. You're never out of love, even if it feels like it. If you feel like you're on the edge with your teenager, go do something that feeds your soul. I love to walk by the ocean. The vastness of it helps me remember that there is a greater power than me running things. I find that by clearing my mind, even while on a short walk, I have a healthier way of approaching things. I relax. I am grateful. I appreciate simple things like the sand under my feet. I also believe music is a powerful tool to replenish your soul's garden. I love to play music and dance around my house like someone without a care in the world. For me it's like a giant vacation that takes place right in the middle of my living room. The energy just shifts; it's amazing.

I love to talk with parents any chance I get. Most parents are on the right track, they just need a vote of confidence.

Three Helpful Tools

1. Talk back to the negative thoughts, the ones that try to convince you that you are running out of kindness. Look for your highest sense of right.

   Parent: "I am so tired of begging you to clean your room. Is it really asking too much?" Or try, "Your room is certainly creative. Perhaps you could draw me a map in case I need to find my way out."

Does this next conversation sound familiar?

Parent "What did you do at school today?"

Child: "Nothing. I'm going to my room."

Parent: "How can you do nothing all day? You must have done something! I want to talk to you!"

Child: "Whatever." (Goes in room and shuts door.)

When frustration tries to rear its short fused head, try reversing your reaction. Remember, unconditional love comes from a limitless supply. Put something yummy on a plate and deliver it to their door. Yes, the same door that just shut you out. Try a simple, "Here, I know you like these cookies, enjoy!"

You're not losing any power or giving in by approaching the above circumstance this way, you're just refusing to engage in negative energy that will lead to nowhere. Love does not fail!

2. Plan a surprise for your child. Make his favorite meal and tell him all the wonderful qualities he has that you admire. It is good for the spirit and your relationship. When you do things to create pleasure and joy, energy builds and happy energy is contagious!

3. Explain to your child when you are having challenges, without worrying them. You certainly don't need to give detailed explanations, but

give them a chance to practice unconditional love. "My job is difficult right now," or "The long hours I'm working make me a bit cranky." Teenagers are amazing and there is no end to their compassion.

Quotes

"The ultimate lesson all of us have to learn is unconditional love, which includes not only others but ourselves, as well."
~ Elizabeth Kubler-Ross

"When your heart is full of love, what room is there for fear?"
~ H. Klemp

"Love is a tool of action; the more we use it the better our skill."
~ Kate Miller

Affirmation

The love that sustains me flows from a limitless source.

A space for you to write your own affirmation

_____

CHAPTER SIX

Children Learn What We Live

I have had a poem in my office for years titled *Children Learn What They Live*. I am sure many of you have read this, but for those who have not, it is wonderful.

> *If a child lives with criticism, he learns to condemn.*
> *If a child lives with hostility, he learns to fight.*
> *If a child lives with ridicule, he learns to be shy.*
> *If a child lives with shame, he learns to be guilty.*
> *If a child lives with tolerance, he learns to be patient.*
> *If a child lives with encouragement, he learns confidence.*
> *If a child lives with praise, he learns to appreciate.*
> *If a child lives with fairness, he learns justice.*
> *If a child lives with security, he learns to have faith.*
> *If a child lives with approval, he learns to like himself.*
> *If a child lives with acceptance and friendship,*
> *He learns to find love in the world.*

~ Unknown

There are many versions of this poem that have been written. I love them all.

Over the last fifteen years I have seen amazing parenting and parenting that has made me weep. By sharing stories from both sides of this journey I hope to offer insight and inspiration.

Story One: *If a Child Lives With Honesty, He Learns to Know Who He Is*

I met the family in this story because the teen had been struggling with underage drinking. This family was well thought of in the community and had the funds to send their child to the best treatment facility that was available. They worked with many professionals over the years. I remember one visit in particular, when their child was eighteen. He explained, "It's hard to not drink when it is everywhere at my house. I can't remember a meal when there were not at least two different kinds of wine on the table. My parents love to talk about wine and take our company to see their wine cellar. My dad said he has a bottle of wine he paid $10,000 for. I guess, growing up, I just always thought I would drink, but never like this."

He told me that when his parents have dinner they always seem to relax after they pour the wine, and that's when the conversation really begins. Because he was eighteen he was allowed to attend the parties his parents hosted in their home. "When the band plays and everyone dances, people are so happy and they are all drinking. It's so much fun to be down there dancing and my friends and I laugh at everybody," he said.

It was difficult for me to explain to him why drinking should not be part of his life. Those he loved and respected were very active players, and he was suffering. I spoke with his parents on several occasions, telling them of his inner struggle. I asked them, if their son was allergic to dogs, would they have dogs running through their home? "Well, don't be silly Kate, of course not," they replied. I said, "That is how alcohol is for your son, like an allergy. He can't be around it, especially in his home." Here was their solution: "He's just not old enough to attend our parties." His mother explained, "We seldom serve alcohol, we just enjoy nice wines and he's obviously not old enough to respect a lovely glass of wine." Her voice was not angry or disrespectful toward her son; she believed what she was saying. What their child actually needed was a lifestyle change that included his entire family.

So on they struggled, in and out of meetings, for years. When the boy was twenty he went away to yet another treatment facility, where he stayed for the next year. His mother called to tell me he was coming home and had done wonderful work there. "I'm sure you are all excited to see him and he can't wait to get home. Please give him my love," I told her. "Oh, yes," she replied, "and what a party we are throwing. He's 21 now, so we don't need to worry about all those drinking problems."

I still remember hanging up the phone feeling overcome with sadness.

Story Two: When Parents Demonstrate Courage, Children Learn to Believe

I once knew a family many years ago that sacrificed everything imaginable for the health of their child. It was never an option to take any other course. You may think this is a decision that any family would make and perhaps that is true, but I feel moved to share their story with you. Stories like this one help on days we feel weak or question the depth of our courage.

They were a family of five living on a small farm in the Midwest. The father was a mechanic by day and a farmer by evening. The mother, a stay at home mom of three children, did the work that needed to be done on the farm during the day, along with her other family responsibilities. Anyone knowing the life of a farm family knows the amount of work it involves.

This particular family worked to pay the doctor bills for their young son and, with very little left, put food on the table. When their son was four years old one of his doctors told them his health might improve if they moved to a higher elevation where the air was much dryer. The doctor did not promise that their son would be well; he said he "hoped". For the parents there was no decision to be made. They explained to their older children what the doctor had told them. They knew they would be leaving friends and family, everything they held dear. For years this family had gathered every weekend at the home of one in-law or the other. Every Sunday each chair was filled at the dining table. This family of five had never been outside their home state for more than a week and the parents had never lived more than thirty minutes from their own parents.

The courage this move took must have been overwhelming. Yet in all the times I have spoken to them about their pioneer journey, they themselves have never mentioned courage. They spoke as if people do it every day. I can't imagine the pain of this young mother, with a sick child, leaving her own mother, moving thousands of miles away. How frightening it must have been for this husband and father to move with one hundred dollars in his pocket and a gas card given to him by his brother. It was up to him to make this all work. Off they drove in their old station wagon, towing a homemade trailer for their very large German Shepherd dog and all of their belongings. They encountered a tornado in Texas that ruined their homemade trailer, which meant they now had their large dog in the back seat of the station wagon.

When they arrived at their destination their stored clothes had been ruined by the storm. They could not afford the prices of homes in the area, so they camped. For three long months they camped to save enough money to rent a house. During their third month of camping a flash flood took most of their camping gear. However, by the time they could afford their first home, their sweet young boy was well. According to his parents, he never again suffered from the illness.

Over the years as they have talked about this pioneer journey west, I have always been amazed that the stories they tell are ones of joy. There were late night games of Yahtzee and swimming in the creek just down the road from their tent home. They spoke of their favorite meals cooked over the camp fire and how dear the Spars Campground was to their hearts.

For me, this story is one of unconditional love and a true sense of responsibility that two parents felt for their child. I was 10 years old when this adventure took place and these courageous people were my parents. I have no memory of worry during our months of camping, just one of great adventure. As a mother of three I have often thought of the courage it took for my parents to accomplish this great move. What I find astonishing is the fact that I remember feeling safe in a home made of canvas and my parents protecting us from the many fears they must have experienced. We were allowed to have a Huck Finn adventure and to me that is great parenting!

Story Three: Sunsets are Orange and Pink, Not Green or *If a Child Lives with Criticism, He Learns to Condemn*

I would like to begin this story by stating that I love teachers. Many of my friends are wonderful teachers and I have friendships with teachers who I met in high school and college. With that said, I would like to use the following story to illustrate the remarkable creative spirit a child naturally has and the responsibility we have as adults and parents to nurture that spirit.

Several years ago I met a young girl. I had been asked by her family to help her through a very difficult time. She was wild, wonderful and respectful. She had brown curly hair, carried a fairy wand almost everywhere and wore white cowboy boots. In fact, her nickname was "Curly". I met very few adults who did not fall in love with her instantly. On Wednesdays I would have the pleasure of meeting Curly at school and walking her home. She had made it very clear on the first visit to my office that she spent all day inside and was sure she would be "much more fun" if we met outside, so I agreed. The first Wednesday of our outdoor meeting I also met her teacher in the classroom. **This woman's critical eye and harsh tones were simply more than I could bear.** It took all of my discipline not to grab my little friend and run screaming out of her classroom. However, I do tend to be a little dramatic (or so I am told), so I decided to let it go and see what the following Wednesday would bring.

The next week I saw my little brown haired fairy sitting alone at a table when I entered her classroom. She looked at me with a fire in her eyes accompanied by tears, a difficult combination to display. I sat down beside her as the other students were lining up to leave the room. "Kate, the sunset is purple, blue and green; I see it that way from inside my eyes, my painting eyes. My teacher threw my paper away and said that sunsets are orange and pink, not green." I assured my friend she must have misunderstood her teacher and that I would wait there until she returned to the classroom so we could get things straightened out.

Well, Curly had reported to me correctly and very soon I found myself in the chair next to my little friend getting the same lecture. "I am sending home a sheet of art paper for her to draw the correct sunset on. She may return it tomorrow. Please try and explain on your walk home the importance of seeing things the way they are. How silly to draw a green sunset." I tried to support Curly's green sunset with my best responses. "The beauty of creativity is vital to the development of a child," was my plea. Oh, how it fell on deaf ears.

I met with the principal and was asked to understand that this particular teacher was about to retire after twenty five years of teaching. "Oh my gosh, how many green sunsets has she thrown out?" I thought. Little by little my friend was losing her zest for green sunsets. What shall I do? We had talked for hours about the wonder of seeing green sunsets and my friend knew exactly where I stood on the subject.

Early in December I went to the school to pick up Curly as usual and the teacher took me outside. "Kate," she said (we were on a first name basis now) "I can't hang up her Santa Clause in the classroom." "Why not?" I gasped. "Look, she made the inside of his pant leg yellow and it looks as though he's gone to the bathroom on himself. Please have her fix it," she replied. "I love her yellow Santa," I said. "I can't ask her to draw him again, it will hurt her feelings." "Feelings have nothing to do with art," her teacher snapped at me.

Choke, gasp, scream! Choke, gasp, scream! I took Curly home and decided from that moment on to have our own art class on Wednesdays. "Whatever you do at school, if you would like, we will do again when we get to your house. You can see it through your 'art eyes' and then draw it," I told her. Curly loved the idea and she couldn't wait to get home to create her own version of orange and pink sunsets. One day we taped poster board to the side of her patio fence and she flung paint at it for an hour. She laughed and I laughed.

When we were finished she said, "Kate, do you think I should invite my teacher to throw paint? It might cheer her up and then she can make yellow Santas." "That is a great idea Curly, a great idea!" I enthused. Her teacher declined the offer. I explained to Curly that some people just hadn't learned to see green sunsets or yellow Santas. I told her the story of Pollyanna, the little girl who found a happy thought in the midst of many grumpy people, and that she was Pollyanna to many people. She loved the story of Pollyanna and managed to complete her year of first grade just fine. Curly learned to have compassion for her teacher; what an amazing little girl! This story was one of the experiences I spoke of earlier that made me weep. Just think of the lives we can touch if we take the time to discover our own green sunsets and yellow Santas.

I have often thought about the responsibility of a parent serving as a role model to their children. How vital it is to stay open to the magic of individual creativity. In lectures I have given, when I say "Parents are the most important role model in the lives of their children", people always nod in agreement. But if you really think about this, it is a huge commitment.

Arriving on time has always been very important to me. If I asked the kids to be home by 6:30, then 6:30 it was. It may have been a bit selfish, but I wanted to know they were home safe, and being on time reduced worry. It also taught respect for other people's time. I became very aware of getting home from my office on time. I recall one evening my daughter was upset because I was twenty minutes late. "Your late mom, you really need to call, I was worried about you." She was right.

Another biggie on my list was no horror movies in our home. This one was a constant battle, but one I would not budge on. Language, distorted images, fears, violence, out of control behaviors; I wasn't going to support any of this. I remember explaining this to a client. It was regarding a movie her son wanted to see and she felt strongly that he should not watch it. She also felt intimidated by the argument he was going to insist on having. I said to her, "Ask your son the following question: 'If someone came to our front door with a chainsaw and a mask on his face, screaming 'Let me in so I can chase you with my chain saw and have you for lunch', would you let him in?'" I believe "NO" is going to be his answer. For me, that is how strongly I felt about allowing those images to be part of our home. My kids would say, "Well, when we go to other friends' houses and they watch them, then we can see them there." My reply was, "Yes, you can. I can't control what happens at someone else's house, but I can control what happens in our home." When my oldest child was an adult he thanked me for this rule.

Three Helpful Tools

1. Think about you, your life, and your daily routine. If you could improve one thing what would it be? Perhaps you might decide that when driving your kids to school you will make it a goal to bless the drivers that pull out in front of you or take your parking space. Not giving their behavior any power whatsoever over your morning with your children is a great lesson to demonstrate for your kids.

2. This week make a list of your heroes. Beside each name write down your reason for selecting them. At dinner bring up the topic and share your list. It is important for your children to know why you respect someone and their accomplishments. What has this person done that would qualify them to be on your hero list? This will also stimulate great conversation between you and your teens.

3. This one takes a bit of courage. I once asked my kids, "If you could change one thing about me,

what would you change?" At first they laughed and said, "Nothing, mom." Then I asked again and promised to stay calm. With very loving voices they said, "When we talk about something you feel strongly about and we disagree, you cut us off. It's like we don't get our opinion out because your mind is already made up." They were right! From that moment on I tried very hard to listen without judgment. It opened the doors to some very interesting conversations. I grew through the experience and so did they. There were some topics that were raised that I had extremely strong ideas about, but I listened anyway. They weren't asking me to change my mind, just to hear their ideas.

Quotes

"Before I got married I had six theories
about bringing up children.
Now I have six children and no theories."
~ John Wilmot

"It's not only children who grow, parents do too. As much as
we watch to see what our children do with their lives, they
are watching us to see what we do with ours. I can't tell my
children to reach for the sun. All I can do is reach for it myself."
~ Joyce Maynard

"Every day is a new day. As a parent I will reach
higher today than yesterday to be great at this job."
~ Kate Miller

Affirmation

I embrace myself as a parent and as a person. I listen
for the right answers that honor both you and me.

A space for you to write your own affirmation

_____

CHAPTER SEVEN

I Believe In You

In this chapter we will be taking a journey. It will be creative, inspiring, and perhaps stressful at times. You may find our means of travel a bit unusual; however, by the end of our voyage you will understand, for we will be traveling through the eyes of a child.

This chapter is to remind tired, well-meaning parents that the connection they have to their children reaches beyond words. It is a journey of the hearts, yours and your child's. "How long will you believe in me?" the child asked his parents. "Forever," was their reply, and so our story begins.

"Oh my gosh, mom, you never give up. I have been living in this cozy warm place for eight long months and you have been amazing. I apologize for every uncomfortable moment you have spent because of me. I know I sat on your bladder (whatever that is) and you would take off running to the bathroom. I know you had an upset tummy. I know you had something called indigestion and sleeping was hard for you. I remember the family got together for a skiing vacation, something everyone said you loved to do. You sat by the fire and read a book, even though I heard the doctor tell you it was okay to ski, just take it easy. But what I really think about, mom, is all the times I've heard you say, 'I believe in him.'

"Every time we face a challenge, even when you were in the hospital for a few weeks, you simply smile at everyone and say, 'Oh, I believe in my baby and I can figure this out. I believe in him!' I'm so proud of you, mom. 'Everything is going to be just fine.' That's what you say to me every night. You rub your tummy and say, 'Everything is going to be just fine.'

"Wow... I'm not sure how I got out of my nice warm nest, but all of a sudden I knew it was time to leave. Dad said push and boy did you push. For a moment the doctor questioned you. 'I think you may need some help getting this baby out.' 'Oh I believe in my baby and I can do this just fine,' you said. That was it. Moments later I was looking up at the face of an angel, an angel who said 'Hi, I'm your mommy'. I knew you would be beautiful, Mom, from the first second I heard your voice. You believed in me, mom and dad, and now I'm here.

"Gosh, time flies when you're a baby. People might not realize it, but we have a lot to do. I would have been lost without you, mom and dad. I remember what everyone said when I was fourteen months old. 'He really should be walking.' My aunts and uncles kept putting me between them and encouraging me to walk. They clapped their hands and jumped around saying stuff like 'Walk here to Auntie!' 'No, walk to Uncle!' I was trying so hard to think how to do that. I was watching everyone around me walk; it looked so easy.

"My feet didn't seem to be connected to the rest of my body. Move foot, move. I was concentrating as hard as I could. Should I worry about this walking thing? In the evenings you and dad would gently place me between you and say, 'We believe in you, you will be a great walker; walk when you are ready.' Your voice was so calm, mom; I could tell you were proud of me even though I hadn't walked a single step yet. I felt so brave, like I could do anything, even walk, and one day I did. I remember your face, mom, you had a huge smile and dad was hugging me. I did it! I walked! You never doubted me, not for one minute, mom. I love you and dad so much.

"I am sure happy you and dad believe in me because being two is tough. I was thinking about this in bed the other night. I heard you and dad say, 'He was certainly busy today, but I believe we will all get through this,' and then you gave one of those great sighs. I love it when you make that noise; it kind of makes me sleepy.

"I'm not sure why I want to figure out what everything is. One minute I am playing with my toys and the next minute I have to know exactly what happens if I turn my cup upside down, so I do it. I sure found out. Moms run. I love it when you run, mom. I hope I can run like you. Maybe if I keep turning my cups upside down and I watch you real carefully, I will learn to be a great runner like you.

"Where did this quiet time chair come from? It is a horrible idea. If you didn't sit me in it I would not have to yell so loud. It seems to be at the times I'm feeling the greatest that I end up in the quiet chair. Yesterday when I was flying around the house chasing the cat and I got his tail it made me laugh so hard. Did you hear how loud the cat meows? I have been watching that cat for months and I knew one day I would catch him. It was a great moment for me, mom, and how did it end? It ended with the quiet chair and me thinking about being gentle with the kitty. Boy, that's not as much fun as chasing, mom.

"And while I'm talking about some of my accomplishments I wanted to mention watching my shoes sailing across the room and making that great loud bang on the windows. Do you know how long it took me to hold those shoe laces just right so my shoes would fly? And what happened? The quiet chair. Sometimes you and dad need to relax and throw shoes with me, then you will understand how much fun it can be. But at the end of my quiet chair time I love what you say to me mom. 'I believe you have had time to think some wonderful quiet thoughts', then you kiss me and hug me and I think, 'I believe in you, mom.'

"I don't think turning four is a good idea. You and dad were talking about a school for four year olds. You said there would be a lot of kids there and I would love it. I don't need a bunch of kids, mom; I just need you and my dad, grandma and the cat; our life is perfect. Do you think grandma will want to go back to school? I thought you and dad finished school. It's very nice of you to go back to school because of me.

"Oh my gosh, you can't be serious, mom. The teacher at that school said I shouldn't worry because she 'would take very good care of me'. I don't need her to take care of me, that's yours and dad's job. I am not going to go to school without you mom, I'm just not. I will scream so loud that I will have to move into the quiet chair forever. I promise you I will never leave you to go to school, don't worry.

"Okay, so just because we are in the driveway of the school doesn't mean I'm getting out of our car. I am going to hang on to this door and no one will pull me off. I'm so scared to leave you, mom. I don't ever want to be away from you. 'I believe you can do this or I would not ask you to,' you said. Those words are gonna make me cry, mom. I know if you believe in me I can learn to do it, I just don't want to. I remember trying to walk. It was so hard. Everyone told me to do it. You told me you believed I could do it and when I was ready, I'd be a great walker. If you say I am okay to go into school, mom, then I will try. Hold my hand, mom, okay, hold it really tight.

"Last night I couldn't sleep because I was so nervous about first grade. I heard my door open and there stood you and dad. I was so happy to see you. You said the magic words, mom, 'We believe in you, you are going to be wonderful in first grade'. If you know that, mom, then I know it too.

"Starting first grade is a huge step for me. I'm really worried about doing everything right. There is a lot to remember in first grade. I have a back pack, lunch money, homework, recess. First grade feels hard. I'm sure happy mom and dad sent me to preschool. I had to be so brave to leave my family, but it was sure fun. I met my best friend Josh there. Josh likes everything I like, chasing cats, watching movies, and digging big holes in his yard; yep, Josh is my best friend.

"Who would have thought that the first day of fourth grade I would be in the principal's office? I can't believe how far that rock flew. All my friends tried really hard to knock that pine cone off the branch, but my rock hit it and down it came. It wasn't my fault the new girl decided to stand under our tree! She could have stood under any tree on the playground, but no, she had to stand under our tree. My friends and I always meet under that tree and decide what we're going to do at recess. I tried to explain to the principal that she was under the wrong tree. He wasn't one bit happy for me that, out of all my friends, I was the one who knocked down the pinecone. The new girl wasn't hurt and I told her I was sorry. He said he had to call you and dad because I was throwing rocks. It reminded me of when I was little, mom, and I had to go to the quiet chair for catching the cat. It was one of the best days of my life, but you told me that's not how the cat felt. The principal told me that's not how the girl felt.

"I could hear through the door of his office when you and dad were talking to him. I was scared until I saw you walk into my school. Somehow I knew everything was going to be okay. I knew you and dad weren't real happy by the way you were pressing your lips together, but I figured you would work that out. You said 'We know our son should not have been playing with rocks and we will be sure he understands what has happened. We also know our son is a good thinker and we believe he will learn an important lesson by today's event.' I remember how happy you were that the girl was not hurt and you said you would have me write a letter of apology. Mom, I also heard you say you believe in me and now I think I might cry. You and dad are the best in the whole world.

"Middle school has its own baseball team. I have been waiting all my life to play baseball. I can see the field from our back yard and now I get to try out. I am so scared, dad. What if I don't make the team? This is my dream. If I try out and the coach tells me I can't play, I don't know what I will do. This is the biggest day of my life. You and mom got me all this new stuff to practice with just so I would be ready for today. I'm so scared. I don't think I can move. I sat on the porch last night looking at that baseball field. When I was little I use to pretend they were calling my name when someone would hit a home run.

"My whole life you told me I could do anything if I believed in me. Today it feels really hard to believe in me. Wait a minute; I can hear you and mom talking about me right now. I learned this trick a long time ago. If I sit at the top of the stairs I can hear lots of conversations. 'He loves baseball and has practiced for years. We feel confident he will do well. The reason we are so excited has nothing to do with baseball. Whether or not our son is put on a baseball team today does not change the wonderful boy he is. Baseball is a game. I believe he will excel at whatever he has passion for in life. That is who he is.'

"'How can I face my parents? Please don't call them, officer, please. My parents didn't do it, I did. Just give me the ticket and I will do whatever you tell me to do. You don't understand, officer, my parents are going to be so disappointed.' The officer said 'You decided to involve your parents when you and your friends decided to drink beer in the park, and you're only seventeen. You also rode here with a friend who's been drinking since you arrived. Who was going to drive that car if you're all drinking beer right now? The fact that your buddy said you were celebrating because you won your game tells me you all need to take a serious look at the way you are making your decisions. I believe you are making some very poor choices.'

"I have never heard those words used like that. The word *believe* belongs to my parents and me. Never in my life has that word made me feel this way. I feel horrible. I have been making a lot of choices in the past year that haven't made me feel very good. I like hanging out with my friends. I notice a lot of them don't have the same feelings about their parents as I do, but that doesn't mean they aren't good friends. I also notice they take risks I really don't want to take.

"Here I am sitting in a police station, waiting for my parents to pick me up. If I can just make them understand that I don't want to mess up anymore. If they will believe in me, just once more, I know I can fix this. I never realized how much I need my parents to believe in me. It can't be too late. Some of my friends have smiles on their faces, like they think all this is funny or something. I just feel sick.

"Mom, as the door opens to the room I'm in I can see you have been crying. Dad looks sad and is holding your hand. I can't believe the first words out of your mouths. 'Are you okay? Are you sure you're okay?' I feel so sad. Your faces have a look I have never seen. You're afraid. The police officer speaks to you for a long time. He tells you that I am making bad choices and he has seen a million kids like me. He tells you that if I stay on this path I will end up in jail. I can't stand it. You guys have to listen to this stranger telling them about your own son. You know me. You know I won't end up in jail. You know I am good. Please, mom, tell him you know I'm not going to end up in jail. Please don't believe I haven't listened to you and dad.

I love you, mom. I love you, dad. He told me not to talk or I would tell you right now. Oh, mom, don't cry. I'm not like all the other kids. I'm me, your son. I know right from wrong. Let me show you, please, let me show you.

"Three years have passed since that awful night and I am now twenty years old and in my third year of college. The words you spoke that night, mom, will stay with me for the rest of my life. 'Our son made a poor choice tonight; it could have been very dangerous. His father and I will face this with him. But it is important to us that he understands that he is not this event. We believe in his ability to do what is right and good. We will climb this mountain together and go forward from here.' That was the last time I made a choice like that. I believe it is because of the endless support of you, mom and dad. I believe in me, that is what I truly believe."

Three Helpful Tools

1. Sit with your teen and tell them all the wonderful things they have accomplished. Begin at the beginning. Say things like, "You were so excited when learned to walk. You could write your name by the age of four. You favorite color was green and every picture you drew when you were five was green. I loved them, that is why I have saved them. You are my same wonderful child and I believe in you now just as I did when you were learning to walk."

2. Here is a great example of a conversation to have with your teen when they need to connect with their confidence. For example, "The other day I was faced with a difficult challenge and I needed

courage. I thought of you. I remembered an incident when you were six and wanted to play ball with the older kids on our block. You took a huge breath and marched out the door. You felt so brave and I was amazed at your confidence. You came in the house that evening a bit taller than when you left." Remind them of who they are!!! This exercise leaves both of you feeling wonderful.

3. Take twenty minutes to rediscover the importance of humor. As mentioned in Tool #1, revisit your teen's childhood. Take this opportunity to talk about their sense of humor. Give them examples of the funny ways they handled things as a child. When my oldest daughter was young and wanted me to know she felt very strongly about something, she ended her sentences with "Really, mommy, really, really, really." Even if her point was that of a five year old, I assure you that I believed in her ability to do whatever she was trying to accomplish. I believed in her, as I still do.

Quotes

"When you believe in a thing, believe in it all the way, implicitly and unquestionably."
~ Walt Disney

"You can do it if you believe you can."
~ Napoleon Hill

"Believing in the passions and possibilities of your teen is a thrilling adventure."

~ Kate Miller

Affirmation

I believe in you. You are wonderful and amazing.
I believe in me. I am wonderful and amazing.
I believe in us. We are wonderful and amazing.

A space for you to write your own affirmation

CHAPTER EIGHT

Sometimes It Takes a Village to Save a Child

When I think of all the wonderful people willing to help teenagers I am overwhelmed. I am a board member of Impact For Youth, a national organization whose goal is to educate students and parents on the dangers of drugs and alcohol. President Janet Meyer and Assistant Director Lori Aiello are the leaders of this village, spending hundreds of hours supporting teens and parents. Day after day they are in their office, waiting to serve. Counselors, teachers, police officers, neighbors, grocery clerks, all are members of villages waiting to serve. I have never asked for support and not found an open heart in every form of village. Isn't that wonderful! Sometimes I had to ask several villagers from different walks of life, but I asked until I found the help that was needed to save a child.

Oftentimes I meet parents who feel that by asking for help they are lacking a skill they should naturally possess. I once felt that way. There is no truth to that statement. We all have our fields of expertise and the world needs each and every one of our wonderful ideas. Those who have spent their time studying and offering classes in parent education are often parents themselves. Their goal is to help you and your children have a strong and happy relationship.

I would like to give an example of the strength that can occur when we ask for the help we need for our children. In some situations this may include many people, in other circumstances it may just be that one perfect person.

Saving Teehan

Teehan was twelve. He lived in a small village with his mother, father, grandparents and many close neighbors. His village was miles from the nearest town. This small village was the only way of life he had ever known. The villagers worked hard to get things done. Each day the teenagers helped in the fields after their teacher, who was also Teehan's grandmother, finished teaching their lessons. They had dreams of leaving the village one day and exploring the world. They studied hard and played hard.

As evening approached, the boys in the village would gather and walk to the river, filling pots with water for the following day. They looked forward to this task, as it somehow always turned into a great adventure. There was only one place on their walk the boys could not go and that was near the abandoned well. Years ago a man had come to their village to drill for water, but with no luck, and now there remained an empty, deep, dark hole. The boys were frightened of the hole. Stories were told of huge snakes and spiders living at the bottom of the well. "My grandfather said they can eat your leg off in one bite," Teehan said. The boys laughed nervously and ran on their way.

One particular day the village was full of excitement. All the villages from miles around were going to town to gather supplies and visit with friends. This trip happened only twice a year, so expectations were high that the week in the city would be filled with excitement.

This year Teehan had decided to stay home with his grandfather, who was very old and weak. Teehan knew his grandmother wanted very badly to go to town and speak with the doctor to see if he could help her husband of fifty-four years. As sad as Teehan was to watch the others leave, he was excited to have his grandfather all to himself. Grandfather was the village storyteller and Teehan knew they would spend long hours laying under the shade of the banana tree, telling stories and eating treats that were supposed to be saved for special occasions.

With so few people in the village, the water supply had lasted longer than usual. Early one afternoon Teehan decided he should again make the trip to the river. "How fast do you think I can run to the river, Grandfather?" "Faster than any boy ever has, Teehan," was his reply. "Okay Grandfather, count until I return and tell me what number I return on." "Ready, go!" said Grandfather. Teehan felt as though he could fly like the wind.

As he ran Teehan's mind was filled with stories from his Grandfather, stories of courage and knowledge. Grandfather had told the story of Thomas, the man who lived in their village five hundred years ago. Thomas was the strongest man in the world. He had carried each boulder that surrounded the village down from the mountain by hand. Grandfather had said the boulders must have each been as heavy as twenty men. As Teehan ran he shouted, "I am Strong Thomas, the strongest man in the world!" Over and over he shouted, leaping and running down the path to the river.

Once at the river, Teehan filled the large pot with water. He suddenly felt very tired. "I wonder if Strong Thomas was tired after he carried rocks all day. I know," he thought, "I will take the short cut home. I will surprise Grandfather at how quickly I can return, even when I am carrying this heavy pot."

Suddenly a cry rang out in the jungle. "AHHHHH!!!" Teehan screamed. He had been so busy thinking about the stories of the day that he had forgotten about the dry well. He fell so far so fast that he checked to see if he was breathing when he hit the bottom. Once he realized he was alive, Teehan wondered if he had lived only to be eaten by a giant spider or snake. "I must yell so that my grandfather can hear me," he thought.

As Grandfather lay by the early evening campfire he heard a sound in the distance. "Someone is yelling for help. It is Teehan! Something is wrong. I must find him," he thought. Grandfather had been bedridden for weeks. He walked only when he needed to. His weakness was more than he could bear at times, but at this moment he did not think of his shaking legs.

"I am coming Teehan, yell again so I can find you! Yell!" As Grandfather moved down the trail to the river his heart sank. "Teehan has fallen into the well," he thought to himself. He left the path, hurrying over the rough terrain leading to the opening of the well. "Teehan my boy, are you okay?" "My foot is hurt, and I am scared, Grandfather." "I will get help, Teehan; I will find a way to get you out of the well. You will have to be very brave because I must go find help. We need a long, strong rope to pull you out. We do not have a rope like that here in our village. I am going to walk to the village at the edge of the meadow. They will have a rope." "Grandfather, you are weak. I am worried for you." "Do not worry. I will find all the strength I need to help you."

Grandfather walked with a spirit in his step he had not felt for a long time. "If I can walk quickly I can reach our neighbors in just a few hours. It will be dark soon. I must hurry," he thought. When the neighboring village was in sight Grandfather began to yell for help. The villagers came running at the sound of urgency in the old man's voice. "My grandson has fallen into a very deep hole. We need a long, strong rope to pull him out. Please help me," Grandfather implored.

"We do not have such a rope, but we will gather all the men in our village and we will all go to the well. There must be a way we can rescue this boy if we all work together. For now, your grandson needs you. Here, take four of our strongest men with you to help. Return quickly to your grandson. He must be very frightened," a village leader said. The neighbors carefully placed Grandfather on a hammock made of straw. Each of the four strong men took one corner. "We will send some men to carry torches. As night falls you will need the fire to reassure your grandson that he is safe," the leader added. "Thank you!" cried Grandfather, and off they went.

As night fell Grandfather heard a sound like thunder. "What is that sound, Teehan? Do you hear it down there?" "Yes, I hear it. What is it, Grandfather? What is happening?" Grandfather stood on top of the rocks piled next to the well. He could not believe his eyes. "It is all of our neighbors; they are coming to help us!" The villagers ran toward Grandfather and Teehan. There were men who were carpenters and men who helped work in the fields. There were leaders of the villages and those who stood watch at night. There were fishermen and cooks. There were women carrying babies on their backs. All had come to help get Teehan out of the well.

"Grandfather, do they have the rope?" Teehan asked. One of the women spoke, "We will be your rope, Teehan, all of us together, and we will lift you out of the well."

One of the villagers lay at the edge of the well. His brother, a carpenter, took hold of his ankles. A farmer took hold of the carpenter's ankles and one by one they lay on the ground, lowering one man at a time down into the well to save Teehan. "Jump into my arms, Teehan, hold on tight, and we will help you out of the well," said the man whose hands were reaching for him in the well. Teehan grabbed the man's neck. "I have him!" shouted the villager. The men above began to pull. Harder and harder they pulled, until each man was out of the well, including dear Teehan.

"How can I ever thank you," Grandfather said to the villagers as he held Teehan in his arms. "You have all worked so hard for a boy you have never met. I will be grateful to each of you for the rest of my life." The carpenter spoke. "We don't have to know Teehan to love him. He is a child, we are adults. It is our job to reach out to children, to lift them out of darkness. It doesn't matter how or why they have fallen into the well, it only matters that we all work together to pull them out."

As the villagers headed home, torches lighting the night sky, Teehan and Grandfather walked slowly toward their village - comforted by the gathering of their new found friends.

In the above story it took the talent of all the villagers to help Teehan. It worked! Everyone gave their time, energy and love. The result was a healthy, safe boy.

There are so many great villages among us. A great example is a college. If it is age appropriate show your child the wonderful opportunities that lie ahead by visiting a college they may be interested in. If their grades are low right now, don't mention it; they know it. Just give them a peak at what the future can hold. Oftentimes by connecting our kids to new opportunities they find new energy for the present moment. There are great questionnaires kids can fill out to help them focus their interests, a type of career counseling. Students usually like this because it is total focus on them. Become an investigator for your child. Ask questions. Search for answers. Remember there is always a way out of the well.

A great way to be part of a village is by joining community boards. Many of the amazing people in my life I met by volunteering on these boards. I also love the afterschool programs that offer tutoring for students. Even if your child is a great student, you meet other wonderful, supportive parents by volunteering to tutor a day or two after school.

I once met a young man who was fourteen. He had made some difficult decisions that had led him to my office. He was required to do sixty hours of community service. Because he was quite shy, I asked our librarian if he might serve his hours there. She said yes. He was such a great fit to their village they hired him as a part time employee. That dear boy told me many months later that the people at the library had saved his life. He explained that he went home to an empty house every day. "Even when my dad gets home he doesn't care if I'm there or not. I think if I didn't show up for weeks he wouldn't notice. I stay at the library until it closes because they care about me there. Now I work there and I go every day. I can handle things a lot better now. They really care about me." I had no idea, when assigning community service to that young man, the strength he would find within that kind and welcoming village. Amazing!

Three Helpful Tools

1. Talk with your teen about the importance of reaching out to others when faced with challenges. This demonstrates a healthy way of living in and connecting to one's community. Reassure your teen that there are many people who have already traveled their road in one way or another and they

are happy to listen and support. If you do decide to ask for help be sure it is a comfortable match for your teen. They need to have a good connection with the person they are going to be working with. Don't be afraid to meet a few counselors and then make a choice.

2. Make a personal list or write a paragraph of what you really want to accomplish with your teen. This helps you decide if it is something that can be handled between you and your teen or if you need the support of a village. Often we need to pinpoint what it is that seems to be bothering us. I once spoke with a mother of a fourteen year old. She poured out her heart with a long list of fears she had about her daughter. I asked her to take that list and condense it, writing only those concerns that were not related to each other. She had only two lines remaining: a) My daughter doesn't talk to me the way she used to, and b) I miss her. Now the mother had something to work with.

3. Become aware of the programs that are in your community. Many high school websites have calendars of events that are teen informative. Invite a group of kids to your house on a Sunday afternoon for food and conversation. Let the kids decide on a topic and give everyone fifteen minutes to explain their feelings. Then have a great open discussion. If your teen laughs at the idea ask them to just try it once. Kids love the attention, and what teenager does not like

the idea of speaking for fifteen minutes with no interruptions!

Quotes

*"The person who sends out positive thoughts
activates the world around him positively
and draws back to himself positive results."*
~ Norman Vincent Peale

*"Asking is the beginning of receiving. Make sure you
don't go to the ocean with only a teaspoon."*
~ Jim Rohn

*"With open arms and hearts of compassion,
your friends who you have not yet met
are waiting to greet you."*
~ Kate Miller

Affirmation

I lovingly embrace the support of my community.
I offer my strengths and accept with
gratitude its knowledge and offerings.

A space for you to write your own affirmation

CHAPTER NINE

Taking Care of You

The father of a fifteen year old girl sat in my office shaking his head and sighing. "I stayed up until midnight the last three nights just making sure my daughter's assignments were complete. If she doesn't complete those assignments she can't play basketball. If she can't play basketball I don't know what she will do. Man, am I tired." He continued, "This reminds me of last year when she wasn't going to play ball because she didn't dress out in PE. That was a tough time for her. I can remember driving home from work hoping she had done what she was supposed to do at school so I wouldn't have to argue with her all night."

"When was the last time you stayed up late doing something for you?" I asked. "Oh, I don't remember. I'm too tired to think about that," he replied. I said, "Then here is your next assignment. By the time I see you next week I want you to have spent two hours doing something you love to do." "But, but, but…" "No 'buts' about this; you need to feed your soul!" I urged.

Pointing to his rather full figured stomach he replied, "Oh I think I feed myself plenty." "I'm not talking about that kind of food. What did you do before you were pushing your daughter to do her homework every night? What did you love to do before you were a parent? What is your favorite drive to take, a place that is so beautiful you forget all those worries? We all have at least one thing that makes us remember who we are. If you put your daughter and her challenges inside a very safe bubble for just a few hours, what would you do?"

His answer was great. "I would find a place to ballroom dance. For years I would go on Saturday evenings and dance for hours. I was pretty good too."

"You are smiling and I see some energy coming through those eyes that isn't the least bit tired. That's what it means to feed your soul. So, this week you must find a place where you can dance. I know of two places locally if you can't find a group. It makes you a better parent, and a better friend to yourself. You have to have balance, and right now your daughter is getting all of you. There is nothing left for you as a person, as a man."

He mused, "I haven't thought about dancing since my wife left. That was twelve years ago. I've been so worried about being a mom and a dad I forgot about dancing. And fishing, I love to go fishing. I used to take my daughter when she was younger, but once she hit ten she let me know she was not touching those worms. Hey, maybe Saturday afternoon when my daughter is at her friend's house I will go fishing. I've always loved that drive to the lake."

This dear man changed right before my eyes. He understood that in no way did this take away from his devoted parenting skills. He reported back to me that not only was he happier, but he was a more patient and joyful parent. He gained confidence from caring for himself and met some nice friends with the same interests. It was a win-win situation.

Now what about the daughter who didn't want to do her homework? When her dad stepped back from his place of worry and was enjoying life a bit more, he understood a very important concept. If he was to stay up all night every night hovering over his daughter, it would never give her the skills she needed to take responsibility for her actions. His job as a parent was to encourage his daughter. It was to provide her a safe and healthy environment to study in. It was to assist her if she needed help by taking her to the library for reference books or having access to the Internet. He could meet with teachers to find out how he could best support what they were striving to accomplish. But most importantly, he demonstrated his belief in her ability to do great things, and she did. Because he allowed her to understand cause and effect, she did miss her first three games that year. He allowed her to understand that basketball was her sport, not his. If she really wanted to play, nothing would stand in her way. I believe she understood that at around game four! What a great gift he gave his daughter, the ability to take control of her life. She graduated from high school and continued to play basketball as a college student.

You and your child are not so different from the above story. Whatever the challenge your child is facing, he or she must face it. And you must keep enough of you to remember who you are. An hour or two away can seem like a mini vacation some days. You deserve it. If you have trouble grasping this concept, ask yourself this question: "If I don't take care of me, who will?" I always tell my teens that they are their own best friend - that goes for parents too.

I was in a restaurant the other day and overheard our waitress talking. "I have a sixteen year old, fourteen year old and six year old. I began taking courses when I was out of high school and I loved it. I am great with numbers and have always wanted to be an accountant." As she spoke about the courses she had taken her eyes lit up, and there was lightheartedness to her spirit. "But then the kids started coming along and I figured I'd just have to wait until they were raised. I can't imagine doing my job here and taking care of the kids and school," she commented.

Yet when she spoke about her course work she had more energy than I had ever seen her have. She smiled at the grades she had made years ago and her character had an unusual strength to it. We frequent this restaurant at least once a week, so I had gotten to know her quite well. She was remembering her dream. As she remembered her dream, she remembered the feelings that went with it. I wanted to jump out of my seat and shout, "You are still the same person and you can do it! Let's figure out a way! You don't have to wait ten years to be living your dream; you just think that you do. It still lights you up, it is still very much a part of you!"

I sat quietly for a bit thinking about this kind lady and how sad it was that she had set her dream aside. I wondered if she felt the difference inside as she spoke about things that lit her up and things that tried to dowse her flame. It was obvious that she loved her children and worked very hard to provide for them. One course, even online, would reconnect her to that hope that lives within us all. I said, "I didn't mean to eavesdrop, but I heard you mention accounting. I think anyone who is good with numbers is a gifted person!" I wanted to see if she was open to the idea of moving forward. I said, "There are great online courses for busy moms and dads these days. Maybe a course or two could keep you moving in that direction. The world certainly needs great accountants." She smiled sweetly and thanked me, but said she was just too tired at the end of the day.

I understand tired. I went to school after having my second child and finished after my third child. I can remember one morning waking up with all three kids sleeping on the couch next to me, my books piled on top of our little sleeping family. That was not an unusual sight in our home. I'm not saying that I had more energy than my friend the waitress. I am saying that I had a great cheering section and I surrounded myself with people who believed in my talents. When I would cry from being tired, someone would say just the right thing to keep me going.

If you have a friend who reminds you of my friend at the restaurant, become their cheerleader. It might be that your energy is just what they need. You will be amazed at the amount of joy you will find by reconnecting yourself or someone else to their dreams.

While we are on the subject of taking care of you, I think it is important to warn you of the dreaded dream snatchers. They can be deadly and can strike anywhere, anytime. Mike was a mechanic working in a small shop that is owned by his brother. He didn't like his brother Frank or working on cars. He worked in the shop because, in Mike's own words, "Hey it's my brother's shop. What is he going to do, fire me if I mess up? Now that would sure start some family trouble."

When Mike was younger he had one dream and one dream only: To be a police officer. He had applied to the academy and did very well until he had to pass the physical agility test. Mike wasn't strong enough to do what was required so he was told to work hard and gain physical strength. He was encouraged to reapply and under no conditions did this situation ruin his chances of being a fine police officer. Mike had always had a bit of an unhealthy ego. He was famous for making fun of kids who couldn't run fast, who were overweight or challenged in some way. He wasn't well liked because of this personality trait. When he was asked to improve his physical ability so that he might be strong enough to live his lifelong dream, he became very bitter. Instead of embracing this valuable information, he made fun of it. Customers dreaded having Mike work on their cars because he was so negative. He allowed no one to be happy for very long, especially his brother, Frank.

Frank is a kindhearted guy who would give you the shirt off his back. When he was little he took everything and anything apart just to see if he could put it back together. By the time Frank was fourteen he was making money fixing bicycles in his backyard. You could hear him laughing as you passed by his house, just enjoying his life working on bicycles. When his brother didn't get into the police department, Frank felt sorry for him. He had encouraged Mike to go to the gym and even offered to pay for his membership. Mike was too angry to accept any help.

As time passed Frank's footsteps began to grow heavy. He loved being a mechanic yet many days dreaded going to his shop. He remembered his days in the backyard working on bikes. He remembered the first day he opened his shop. It had been a grand opening that was indeed the talk of their small Midwest town. There he stood looking at the sign above the garage: FRANK'S AUTO REPAIR - WELCOME. Frank's wife had made her famous apple pies and his sisters had decorated the parking lot. He recalled the feelings of those early days in his shop and wondered where his excitement had gone.

As he sat quietly in his office he overheard Mike talking to one of his customers. "Yeah, I bet this is going to cost you an arm and a leg. The only thing worse than an attorney is a mechanic. It's hard for me to believe this is my brother's dream. Can you imagine growing up saying 'When I grow up I want to be a mechanic'? If the police department wasn't so lame I would have let them hire me. Oh well, their loss. My brother will call you in the morning and let you know the damage that we have caused."

Frank's heart was heavy knowing what he had to do. He could not remember how many times he had talked to Mike about being positive with his customers. At the end of the work day he gave his brother a month's pay, wished him well and told him he no longer had a job in his shop. He was as kind as he could be, but he knew he had to protect what was so dear to him, his dream, the food his soul lived on. Once his brother was gone, he began to reconnect to the joys of his shop and experienced the contentment he first felt in his backyard repairing his friends' bikes.

Mike's dream had become too painful to confront, so he was going to make sure those around him knew that life was not fair and you would most likely end up miserable. Mike was a dream snatcher! Frank wasn't judging Mike for his behavior, but allowing him to work in his shop certainly didn't make Mike face himself very honestly. Firing Mike was the best gift Frank could give to both himself and Mike.

Three Helpful Tools

1. Do you remember resting your chin on the open window of the car as your parents drove? The wind is blowing your hair and your eyes are tightly closed. You have a big smile on your face as if there is nothing happening anywhere in the world but right here, right now, as the wind blows on your face. What makes that feeling of contentment inside of you? What brings you the feeling of youthful joy? If your answer does not come quickly then your assignment is to spend

five minutes each day searching your heart, soul and spirit for this feeling, your answer. We all have one, or many. This is to be a lighthearted and relaxing assignment.

2. Just before you fall asleep focus on a vision that fills you with gratitude. It can be something that happened today or years ago. Just see it clearly. Relax and be grateful. The feeling of gratitude is like a mini vacation (and it's free).

3. Interview three of your closest friends or family members. Choose those who know you well and whom you respect and trust. Ask them to describe your unique qualities. Write down their answers and keep them in your pocket or near your bed. Look at them often and rejoice! You are wonderful! Remember Dr. Seuss's quote earlier, "There is no one Youer than You"!

Quotes

*"Diamonds are no more than chunks of
coal that stuck to their jobs."*
~ Malcolm Forbes

"Our lives begin to end the moment we cease to dream."
~ Martin Luther King, Jr.

*"Giving up is never an option. We can rest, cry, pray,
reach out, ask for help, but we may never give up."*
~ Kate Miller

Affirmation

I celebrate and rejoice. As I close my eyes, I
open my heart to the endless possibilities
that are waiting for me. I feel healthy
and excited about my life.

A space for you to write your own affirmation

CHAPTER TEN

An Endless Stream of Hopes and Dreams

As I write this last chapter I am touched by the depth of love I find in parents. When I speak, looking out at my audience, the love on the faces of my families moves me far beyond words. The desire for their children to live safe, joyful and successful lives is endless. Throughout the lives of their children a parent's love seems to flow as an endless stream of hope, moving tirelessly in support of their child's needs and desires.

When children are born we look at them through the eyes of limitless possibilities. Before they have spoken a single word we believe in their ability to accomplish anything their heart desires. Think of the amount of hope and faith we are standing on. By holding this amazing, beautiful baby, we believe their future holds no boundaries. Hmm… where is that feeling by their fifteenth birthday? It is there. It is always there. Life happens. The stream varies in strength at times, but it continues. Rains fall and the stream is full and vibrant. Drought comes and only a trickle is visible.

My experience has led me to believe that labels or the thoughts of others have a lot to do with the heaviness both children and parents begin to experience over time. I want to share a story with you of a young girl I had the pleasure of knowing. It is a great example of what labeling does and how a crystal clear stream gets clogged with debris.

Gina was fourteen and a gifted athlete. She was selected to play on her school's varsity basketball team and chosen for a very elite group of high school golfers. She had enjoyed school all of her life and never given anyone a reason to doubt her ability to make good, healthy decisions. Gina was vibrant, even jolly. She loved life and believed life loved her.

One day after basketball practice her coach took her aside and questioned her about her weight. Gina told me the following: "My coach said, 'You know, Gina, if you'd drop about ten pounds you'd move around the court a lot faster. You're only fourteen years old and on varsity, but by your junior year things might change unless you watch that weight of yours. Besides, skinny is in.'" Gina was embarrassed and morally devastated. There is nothing more damaging than to tell a teenager that their weight is undesirable. In that very moment, Gina said she felt as though "my spirit had left my body. I felt weak and sad. It was the worst feeling of my life." Although some people might be able to take this kind of criticism, I have met very few of them. Because this was seen as failure to Gina, and embarrassing, she told no one. Gina embraced this judgment as a true fact about who she was. She let it take her over.

Gina took matters into her own hands. She bought diet pills. When diet pills didn't do the trick she opted for stronger drugs, guaranteed to kill her appetite. Because she was now altering the chemistry of her own wonderful, perfect, God given, gifted body, Gina began to change. She couldn't sleep because the pills kept her up. She was nervous all the time due to the effects of the drugs. She was not able to concentrate. Her grades began to drop. Gina began associating more with failure than living her dreams. Over a period of time the following labels began being placed on Gina:

"Gina, you are not turning in your homework. It seems like you're not trying."

"Gina, why are you missing basketball practice? Don't you care?"

"I don't like these new friends of yours. None of them are on your basketball team."

"Gina, you've really changed. You're not the student you used to be."

"Gina, if you don't bring up your grades, you won't be eligible to play ball."

"We are taking you off the special golf team, as the members of this team are outstanding students and you're not reaching that standard."

Day by day Gina associated less with her gifts and more with failure. Two of Gina's girlfriends brought her to my office. She told me the whole story. She also told me she "hated" her body. Gina was frozen inside the words of her coach. Gina had parents who loved her. They were kind people who would move mountains for their daughter. They were frightened parents who didn't know this new Gina. They were comfortable with Gina the athlete who always seemed to be in control of her life. They were terrified of Gina the student who didn't turn in her work and had stopped playing basketball. They asked me, "Gina's dream for her life is falling apart and so are we. Where did our daughter go?" "Let's find her," was my reply.

We talked a lot about Gina as a baby and her early years of school. We talked for hours over her accomplishments and how happy she had always been. When the conversation would try to wind its way back to a stream of drought and her recent failures I would turn Gina's parents back toward her successes. "Concentrate on the daughter you know so well. Every time you see her face in your thoughts say, 'There is a healthy, confident Gina who I believe in!' Say it all day long over and over again. 'Gina is not this event! Gina is amazing!'"

I told Gina a story that I have used many times when kids come to me with painful issues that have been given to them by some unthinking person. "Gina," I said, "let's pretend you are sitting on your couch at home having the best evening ever. Your parents just gave you money to go shopping and mom cooked your favorite dinner. All of the sudden there is a knock at the door. You pull back the curtain and see a man standing there with a mask on. It is clear his intention is to harm you and your family. There is a huge lock on your door and he can only get in if you unlock the lock and allow him to enter. You have complete control, Gina. You can save yourself and your family. Do you unlock the door, allowing him to come in, taking everything you hold dear, or do you close the curtain and walk away, knowing that he can never enter your home?"

Gina laughed and said, "Kate, that is ridiculous." "Oh really," was my reply. "Gina, that is what you have allowed your coach to do. He walked in and took everything you hold dear. I'm sure that was not his intention, but that is what is happening. Lock the door, Gina. Just lock it. Send the robber away and let's find your safe, wonderful, successful, playful, Gina life." And that is exactly what she did. We met for a few more visits. Gina went to the doctor, getting the help she needed after using diet drugs, drugs that now held no appeal.

Gina learned to stand guard at the door of her thoughts. She was, and is, in control of what she believes to be true about Gina. Gina owns her dreams.

It was by the words of others that Gina lost her confidence and by the labels placed on her that her parents' stream of hope began to collect debris. They all fought for Gina and for her right to sustain her true self. Patrick Henry said, "I like the dreams of the future better than the history of the past." I agree.

It's easy to understand how parents get slow moving streams. It is also clear that the love they have for their children stands stronger than any dam that would try and block the constant outpouring of parental love. I believe the depth a parent loves their child is magical. I have witnessed parents at the beginning of our meetings say, "That's it, I just give up! I'm tired and I need a break". One hour later, after some great discussion, it goes something like this, "I'm sorry we fought. Let's go have some dinner. Love you lots." Endless streams of love.

I want to support the parent who reads this and says, "What about me? I had to send my child away so they could be in a monitored environment just to keep them safe, just to keep them from using drugs or running away or living on the streets." Sometimes we need to broaden our concept of home. A great treatment center can be an extension of your home. The idea of home is to nurture, embrace and encourage. If this is what is needed to ensure your child's safety, then you have simply broadened your borders of home. Never is a more difficult decision made by parents. It is unconditional love to have to take this step.

I believe strongly that the love I have witnessed over the past many years comes from a bottomless well. This well is filled with hope and dreams and knowledge. It is forgiving and concerned. It is compassionate and sturdy and is not afraid to fight for the rights of its sons and daughters.

I believe in you! Never let anything or anyone tell you that you can't do what is needed to support your child. Fill your heart with gratitude that you are who you are. Rejoice! Praise yourself daily for your dedication toward helping your child build a strong and beautiful life.

Do your daily mantras. Feed your soul. Dance, sing, and give thanks. You are amazing.

Three Helpful Tools

1. Plan a celebration. Call it "A Special Day Celebration". Celebrate everything you love about your teenagers. Bake a cake. Talk about their talents. Leave them a message on their bathroom mirror. Celebrate Love!

2. Place a piece of paper somewhere in the house that is accessible to everyone. For one week, each time anyone in the family hears words of kindness spoken toward someone, write them down. At the end of the week, take your list to the dinner table and read it out loud. Discuss how hearing these kind thoughts makes you feel. It is fun and something everyone can enjoy. If your list is too short it alerts you as a family to actively work on this. Try to double your list from week to week. This process creates a habit. After several weeks and wonderful lists, can you think of a better habit for your family to have?

3. Decide on an adventure you can take on as a family. Perhaps you can sponsor a child in need and everyone can give a small amount of their own money. You can see your love in action. Is there someone in your neighborhood who needs your family's help on Sunday afternoons? Do you have a relative who doesn't get many family visitors? Is there a park by your house that needs attention? Love in action, working together as a family: It brings amazing results.

Quotes

"To love someone is to see a miracle invisible to others."
~ Francois Mauriac

"Love cometh like sunshine after rain."
~ William Shakespeare

"The human heart, at whatever age, opens to the heart that opens in return."
~ Maria Edgeworth

Affirmation

Each day begins brand new. I begin my day by loving you.

A space for you to write your own affirmation

_____